Quail

and Other Galliforms

Book Author: Rob Knight
For World Book:
Editorial: Paul A. Kobasa, Scott Thomas, Christine Sullivan
Research: Cheryl Graham
Graphics and Design: Sandra Dyrlund, Brenda Tropinski
Photos: Tom Evans
Permissions: Janet Peterson
Indexing: David Pofelski
Proofreading: Tina Ramirez
Pre-press and Manufacturing: Carma Fazio, Anne Fritzinger, Steve Hueppchen

**For information about other World Book publications, visit our Web site at
http://www.worldbookonline.com or call 1-800-WORLDBK (967-5325). For information about sales
to schools and libraries, call 1-800-975-3250 (United States); 1-800-837-5365 (Canada).**

World Book, Inc.
233 N. Michigan Avenue
Chicago, IL 60601
U.S.A.

The Library of Congress has cataloged an earlier edition of this title as follows:

Quail and other galliforms.
        p. cm. -- (World Book's animals of the world)
    Includes bibliographical references and index.
    ISBN 0-7166-1266-6
    1. Galliformes--Juvenile literature. 2. Quails--Juvenile literature.
  I. World Book, Inc. II. Series.
  QL696 .G2Q35 2005
  598.6'2--dc22

                                        2004019043

This edition:
Quail: ISBN-10: 0-7166-1338-7   ISBN-13: 978-0-7166-1338-1
Set 4: ISBN-10: 0-7166-1285-2   ISBN-13: 978-0-7166-1285-8

Printed in Malaysia
3 4 5 6 7 8 09 08 07

Picture Acknowledgments: Cover: © Darren Bennett, Animals Animals; © D. Robert & Lorri Franz, Corbis; © Robert Maier,
Animals Animals; © Dale C. Spartas, Corbis; © Roger Wilmshurst, Photo Researchers.

© Jen and Des Bartlett, Bruce Coleman Inc. 5, 15; © Darren Bennett, Animals Animals 5, 9, 45; © Paul & Joyce Berquist,
Animals Animals 3, 61; © Nell Bolen, Photo Researchers 43; © Tom Brakefield, Corbis 25; © Jane Burton, Bruce Coleman Inc.
57; © Peter Cairns, Worldwide Picture Library/Alamy Images 39; © Larry Ditto, Bruce Coleman Inc. 37; © Rick Edwards, Alamy
Images 53; © Kenneth Fink, Bruce Coleman Inc. 27; © D. Robert & Lorri Franz, Corbis 4, 49; © Sumio Harada, Minden Pictures
9; © Eric and David Hosking, Corbis 35; © Byron Jorjorian, Alamy Images 21; © Wayne Lankinen, Bruce Coleman Inc. 7;
© Robert Maier, Animals Animals 9, 23; © Maslowski Photo/Photo Researchers 13, 17; © Hans Reinhard, Bruce Coleman Inc.
51; © H. Reinhard, Okapia/Photo Researchers 29; © Ray Richardson, Animals Animals 47; © Leonard Rue, Animals Animals 41;
© Joel Sartore, National Geographic/Getty Images 33; © Dale C. Spartas, Corbis 55; © Lynn Stone, Bruce Coleman Inc. 59;
© Tom Tietz, Getty Images 19; © Roger Wilmshurst, Photo Researchers 31; © Art Wolfe, Photo Researchers 9.

Illustrations: WORLD BOOK illustration by John Fleck 11.

World Book's Animals of the World

Quail
and Other Galliforms

WORLD
BOOK

a Scott Fetzer company
Chicago
www.worldbookonline.com

Contents

Can you guess why I need such fuzzy feet?

What are all those little dots? I wonder if they taste good...

I have something to grouse about—I am NOT a chicken!

What Are Galliforms?

Galliforms *(GAL uh fawrmz)* are the birds that scientists have grouped into a scientific order called Galliformes *(GAL uh FAWR meez)*. Like most birds, galliforms have feathers and wings. Unlike many other birds, however, galliforms live on the ground.

Quail *(kwayl)* are small galliforms. There are about 45 species, or kinds, of quail. Most adult quail are only 8 to 12 inches (20 to 30 centimeters) long. The heaviest quail weigh only about 8 ounces (230 grams)—the weight of a cup of yogurt!

Like other galliforms, quail live on the ground and build their nests there. They hide these nests behind tall grass. Quail are able to fly. They cannot fly far, though. When quail do fly, it is usually only for a short distance and to get away from a predator, such as a fox.

Other well-known galliforms are chickens, turkeys, and pheasants *(FEHZ uhntz).* Because all these birds are often hunted for sport and for their meat, they are also known as game birds.

Gambel's quail

Where in the World Do Quail and Other Galliforms Live?

Quail live throughout the world. They live on grasslands and in other open habitats on all continents except Antarctica.

All galliforms, including quail, are widespread. The partridge *(PAHR trihj)* lives in Europe, Asia, Africa, and Australia. Grouse *(grous)* live in North America, Europe, and Asia. There are even a few species of galliform that live far north within the Arctic Circle.

Because many species of galliform are hunted for sport, these birds have also been introduced into areas in which they did not originally live. For example, at one time the ring-necked pheasant lived only in parts of Asia. In the late 1800's, people brought this pheasant to Europe and North America. In many of the areas where it was introduced, the ring-necked pheasant still survives.

Blue grouse

European quail

Prairie-chicken

Black partridge

What Is Under
All Those Feathers?

Underneath a quail's feathers are skin, muscles, bones, and organs.

Some of these organs make up the quail's digestive system, which allows the bird to take in and use food. The esophagus *(ee SOF uh guhs)*, crop, gizzard *(GIHZ uhrd),* and small intestine are parts of the quail's digestive system. So are the bird's bill and mouth.

A quail has a heart and brain, too. The heart pumps blood to all parts of the body through the circulatory system. The brain controls the bird's nervous system and behavior.

10

Diagram of a Quail

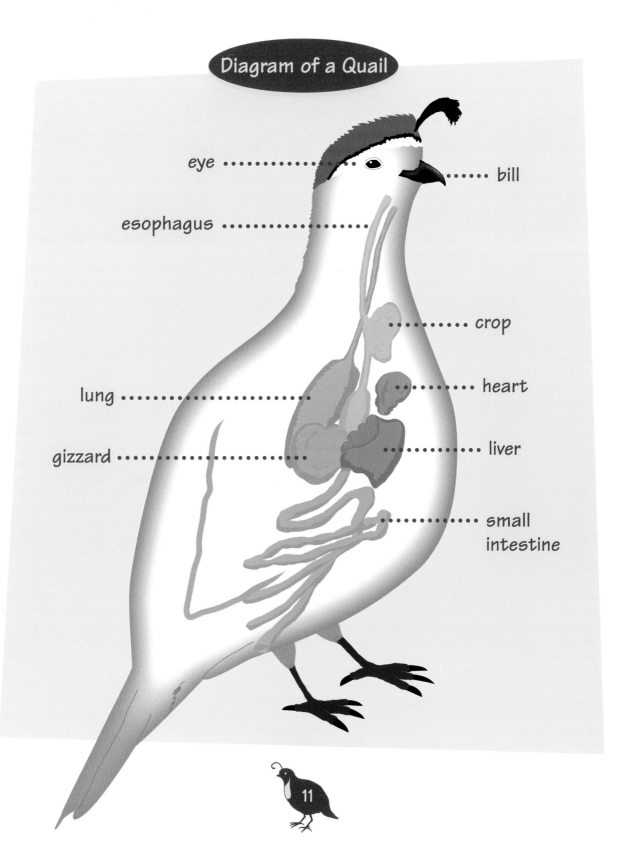

eye

bill

esophagus

crop

heart

lung

liver

gizzard

small
intestine

What's for Dinner If You're a Quail?

Quail are not strong fliers, swimmers, or waders, because they do not need to be. They search for food, or forage, almost entirely on the ground.

Plump quail may look like slow-moving birds, but they have strong legs and are quite nimble on the ground. They also have strong toes, which are perfect for scraping up roots or uncovering fallen seeds. Quail will also reach for low-hanging fruits, flowers, and leaves.

Sometimes, a quail will scrape up or chase after insects, too. Insects are an especially important part of a young quail's diet. Insects contain important nutrients *(NOO tree uhntz),* or nourishment, that the quail needs to grow.

All animals need water as well as food. Quail, however, can live on very little water—as little as one-half teaspoon a day. Quail can get this small amount of water just from the plants they eat.

Bobwhite quail

Why Do Quail Swallow Pebbles and Sand?

When humans eat, they put the food into their mouths. Then they chew the food, using their hard teeth to grind it up, before swallowing it.

Birds do not have teeth. But they have a special way to grind up hard food. They have a gizzard. A gizzard is the strong, muscular part of a bird's digestive system.

Such birds as quail peck at the ground to pick up gravel—small pebbles and bits of sand. A bird swallows the gravel, which ends up in the gizzard. Muscular contractions cause the gizzard to squeeze and re-squeeze its contents. This squeezing causes the small, sharp pieces of gravel to grind up the food in the gizzard. Eventually, a bird passes the gravel as waste. Then the bird needs to swallow more gravel to keep its digestive system working properly.

Gambel's quail

15

How Does a Quail Care for Its Young?

Like other birds, quail build nests in which to lay their eggs. Unlike songbirds, though, quail build their nests on the ground. It might be either the male or the female quail that chooses the nesting spot behind tall grass or bushes. He or she then scrapes a shallow hole and lines it with soft grass and leaves. Then the female lays her eggs in the nest.

The quail brood the eggs—that means they sit on them to keep them warm—until they hatch. Either the male or the female quail may sit on the eggs to warm them. The eggs take from between two and three weeks to hatch.

The newly hatched chicks need protection. As soon as possible, the parents lead their chicks away from the nest. The broken eggshells might make predators hungry for dinner. When danger is near, the quail chicks run to hide under a parent's wing.

Young quail do not need care for very long. They are able to eat food on their own right away. About one week after hatching, they can fly.

Gambel's quail
with young

What Is a Covey of Quail?

A covey *(KUHV ee)* is a name for a flock or group of quail. A covey may have 10 or fewer birds or as many as 100 or more, depending upon the species of quail.

Quail usually form coveys in the fall and winter. During breeding season, the covey breaks up as pairs split off from it to breed and raise their young.

Quail in a covey snuggle together when they roost, or settle down to rest or sleep. Snuggling up to each other's warm bodies keeps the group warm on chilly nights. Some kinds of quail may not actually generate enough warmth individually to survive a cold night.

Quail often search for food in a covey rather than by themselves. Together, they march away from their roosting place to forage in early morning and again in late afternoon. They have a better chance of escaping a predator it they stay in a group. Page 20 will explain how the covey gives protection against predators.

Covey of
bobwhite quail

How Do Quail Escape from Predators?

Because quail cannot fly very well, it is no wonder that they are preyed upon by such animals as foxes, coyotes, and other predators. But, quail have ways to protect themselves, too. When predators come near, quail—which are very fast runners—may run into a thicket where they can escape by staying hidden.

Quail feathers are mostly brown, tan, gray, or white, with a pattern of spots or stripes. These feathers help quail to hide among grass, fallen branches, and leaves. The camouflage *(KAM uh flahzh)* makes it hard for a predator to see the quail.

What happens when a predator comes near a covey? Often, the quail fly straight up, quite suddenly, beating their wings loudly. The noise and motion will often startle the predator, giving the covey time to get away. Humans make use of this behavior when hunting quail. A bird dog first locates the quail for the hunter; when the hunter gives a signal, the dog runs into the covey and flushes them (causes them to fly up). The quail then are an easier target for the hunter.

Camouflaged quail
hiding from bird dog

How Fast Are Quail?

Quail are pretty fast runners for birds. When a quail is in a hurry, it can run about 20 feet (6 meters) in one second. Although a quail would have a hard time outrunning a predator over long distances, it is fast enough to dart out of a predator's grasp and into the thicket.

Although quail fly only for short distances, some can fly quite fast. One of the fastest quail is the California quail. It has been timed flying at speeds of more than 50 miles (80 kilometers) per hour. The northern bobwhite can fly at about 40 miles (64 kilometers) per hour for short flights.

California quail

Who Is Bob White?

Anyone who has visited the countryside is likely to have heard a bird call that sounded like "bob-WHITE."

The bird that makes that call is the northern bobwhite quail. So, that is who Bob White is—a common quail that is found in the central and eastern United States and in Mexico.

The northern bobwhite lives in grasslands and brush areas near forests. It has striking markings on its head. But it does not have a crest, or topknot, as do certain other types of quail, such as the mountain quail.

Northern
bobwhite quail

Why Are Some Galliforms Show-offs?

Some male pheasants have bright, showy feathers. Male turkeys spread out their fans. Male ruffed grouse also open up their fans. These are examples of male bird behaviors called displays. Another galliform with a strange display is the male Bulwer's pheasant. This bird has bright blue areas of skin on its head, called wattles *(WOT uhzl).* He enlarges these wattles during a mating display.

While it seems as if these male birds are just showing off, there is a purpose behind their display behaviors. Male birds use them to attract female birds. The males with the best displays are usually the healthiest and most fit.

Female galliforms are attracted to fit males of their species because these males are often more capable of helping to raise young. In addition to being better able to raise young, healthy parents tend to produce healthy young. That is because, as with other animals, the offspring of birds share the hereditary traits of their parents.

Bulwer's pheasant

Who Has a Big, Showy Fan?

A male Indian peafowl has an extremely large and showy fan. The Indian peafowl is commonly called a peacock.

Actually, the word peacock refers only to the male bird. The female is called a peahen. But most people call either the males or the females peacocks.

A male uses his large fan as a display to attract a mate. When not used for display, the fan feathers trail behind the bird. In this position, the fan feathers are called a train, like the trailing fabric on a bride's gown. Female peafowl do not have fans.

The male's fan is made up of some 200 long feathers. These beautiful feathers can be some 60 inches (about 150 centimeters) in length. They are greenish-blue and feature bold spots that look like eyes. As the peacock displays his fan, he shakes its feathers so that they make a rattling noise. This also helps attract the female's attention.

Indian peacock

29

What Are Pheasants?

Pheasants are a colorful group of galliforms. They are larger and heavier than quail. The males of most species of pheasant have a long tail.

Most kinds of pheasant live in wooded areas. Pheasants often roost in trees at night. Some pheasants, such as the ring-necked pheasant, prefer open areas or forest edges.

Among birds, males are often showier and more colorful than females. This is certainly true of pheasants. For example, the male ring-necked pheasant has a long tail, a colorful head, and beautiful feathers. The female bird has a shorter tail, a plainer head, and less colorful feathers.

Ring-necked pheasant

Who Has a Crown of Gold?

It is the golden pheasant, of course. The male golden pheasant has bright yellow-gold feathers on the top of his head that form his "crown."

The male golden pheasant has many brightly colored feathers on his body, as well. He has a bright red breast and bright blue feathers on his wings. The male's ruff—the layer of feathers that stand out on his neck—looks something like a cape. The bird fans the ruff over his head and beak to attract the female's attention.

This pheasant is found in mountain habitats of Tibet and in central China. But, people have brought this rare and beautiful bird to zoos all over the world.

Golden pheasant

How Can Pheasants Take a Bath in Dust?

When people take a bath, they get into a tub full of water. Many birds take a bath in water, as well. But, when water is not available, some birds take a bath in dust. Pheasants often take dust baths. Some kinds of quail do, too.

People would not feel very clean if they took a dust bath. But birds' bodies are different. Birds are covered with feathers, and those feathers keep a bird warm. But feathers also make a cozy home for lice and other parasites *(PAR uh sytz).* A parasite is an organism that lives on another organism, called a host, sometimes harming the host.

When a bird takes a bath in dust, the powdery dirt goes all through the bird's feathery coat. This helps straighten the feathers, and that makes them better at keeping the bird warm. The powdery dirt may also drive out the insects and other parasites hiding in the feathers.

Golden pheasant
taking a dust bath

Who Comes to Thanksgiving Dinner?

A roasted turkey is a central part of a traditional Thanksgiving or Christmas dinner in many homes throughout the United States and Canada.

The turkey is a large galliform. An adult wild turkey can weigh as much as 16 pounds (7.3 kilograms). Like the peacock, the male turkey—called a tom—can make a big, showy fan with its feathers. A female turkey is called a hen.

Turkeys have no feathers at all on their head or neck. A long, loose piece of skin called a wattle covers the male's lower jaw and neck.

Wild turkeys live in North America, mostly in or near wooded areas. These turkeys can both run and fly. Domestic turkeys—that is, turkeys raised on farms—are found in many parts of the world. Domestic turkeys are bred for their meat. They cannot fly because their wings cannot support their body weight.

Wild turkey

What Are Grouse?

Grouse are quail-like galliforms. Like quail, grouse live mostly on the ground and also nest on the ground.

All grouse live in the Northern Hemisphere (north of the equator). Some live in high mountains or far north in cold places.

An adult grouse is about the size of a large chicken. The feathers covering a grouse's body are usually dull, instead of brightly colored like a pheasant's feathers. Many kinds of grouse have a red or orange growth, called a comb, above each eye. A bird's comb is a featherless patch of puffy, brightly colored skin.

Some types of grouse, like the black grouse, have a ruff, a special layer of feathers on their neck. Male black grouse have a white stripe along each wing. Female black grouse are actually more grayish-brown in color.

38

Male black grouse

Which Kind of Grouse Snacks on Evergreen Needles?

The spruce grouse is named for the food it eats. This grouse eats the thin leaves, called needles, of spruce trees, as well as the needles of other evergreen trees.

The spruce grouse lives in evergreen forests in North America. It spends most of its time in the trees, where it eats needles and small green buds from branches.

Few animals can eat evergreen needles. They are hard to digest, and it is difficult to get nutrients from them. They are even poisonous to some animals. But, the stomach of the spruce grouse can break down needles safely so the bird can use them for food.

Spruce grouse

Can a Grouse
Play the Drums?

Of course, a grouse does not sit at a drum set and play the drums with sticks! But a ruffed grouse can use its wings to make a drumming sound.

To make this sound, a ruffed grouse often perches on a log in the forest. The bird beats its wings back and forth very, very fast. The wings may beat 20 times each second. All of this wing-beating creates a thumping noise. The log amplifies the noise. A male ruffed grouse uses this drumming as a territorial display to keep other male ruffed grouses away.

If you go on a hike in the woods one day, maybe you will hear a drum roll—played by a ruffed grouse!

Male ruffed grouse

43

What Is a Prairie-Chicken?

The prairie-chicken is not really a chicken. Instead, it is a kind of grouse. It is called a prairie-chicken because it resembles a chicken and lives in parts of North America that were once covered with flat or rolling grassland called prairie.

Like other kinds of grouse, the male prairie-chicken likes to "show off." He makes quite a display for female prairie-chickens. He fans his tail feathers. He points the feathers on his head straight up in the air. He also puffs out an orange air sac on each side of his neck. As if that were not enough, he continues his display by making a hooting noise that sounds like air being blown across the top of a bottle!

Male prairie-chicken displaying

What Is a Ptarmigan?

A ptarmigan *(TAHR muh guhn)* is a kind of grouse that lives in cold northern places or high mountains. Such places are covered with snow in winter.

Many galliforms have feathers that help them blend in with grasses and bushes. Ptarmigans have a coat of white feathers in winter to help them blend in with snow. This is called camouflage, and it makes it harder for a hungry fox or owl to find the ptarmigan.

When spring comes and the snow melts, the ptarmigan changes its coat. New feathers that are reddish-brown or black grow in, so that the ptarmigan can blend in with short grasses, rocks, and bushes. Ptarmigans are the only galliforms that "change coats" with the seasons.

Ptarmigan

Do Some Birds Wear Snow Boots?

Ptarmigans spend months living on the cold, snowy ground. But, a ptarmigan has just the right clothing for winter weather. It has a "blanket" of warm feathers and also has warm "snow boots"!

A ptarmigan's boots are not at all like peoples' boots. Instead, the bird has thick bunches of feathers around its feet and legs. The feet of most birds are bare. But a ptarmigan has just the right "boots" for a cold, snowy winter. In spring, the ptarmigan sheds the feathers that protect its feet and legs.

Ptarmigan in snow

What Are Partridges?

Partridges are quail-like birds that live throughout the world. Partridges are usually bigger than most quail but smaller than many grouse. Partridges are about 12 inches (30 centimeters) long.

Perhaps the best-known partridge is the gray, or common, partridge. This partridge originally lived in Europe, Africa, and Asia. But, as with other galliforms, gray partridges were introduced in other regions for sport. Today, gray partridges live in the wild in parts of the northern United States and southern Canada, as well as in their original habitats in the Old World.

Partridges may be found in wild grasslands and in crop fields and pastures. In fields, they find grains of corn, oats, and wheat to eat. They find plenty of tasty insects, too.

Gray partridges

What Are Guineafowl?

The guineafowl *(GIHN ee fowl)* is another relative of quail, pheasants, grouse, and partridges. Wild guineafowl live in Africa. The original guineafowl were from the Gulf of Guinea region of Africa, and that is how they got their name. But, these birds have now been introduced all over the world to be raised for their meat.

As its name suggests, the helmeted guineafowl has a "helmet" on its head. A helmet is a hard hat that construction workers, bike riders, and other people wear to protect their heads. The guineafowl's "helmet" is a hard, bony lump on its head. Male guineafowl will use this bony growth to butt another male that is trying to take its mate.

Guineafowl make very loud cries when they are frightened. So, they are prized for being good "watchdogs" on farms.

Helmeted guineafowl

Who Cries "chu KAHR!"?

The chukar does! In fact, this type of quail gets its name from the call it makes.

Chukars originally lived only in Asia. But like the ring-necked pheasant and the gray partridge, people brought the chukar to North America for sport. Today, many chukars survive in the wild in Canada and the western United States.

Unlike many other birds, the male and female of the species look very similar to one another. They are both fairly small, stocky grayish-blue birds with brownish backs and white bellies. Chukars have a black band above their red bill. The band goes across their face and neck like a mask. They also have red rings around their eyes, and their legs and feet are red, too!

Chukar

How Do Wild Birds Become Farm Animals?

Although the red junglefowl may look a lot like a domestic chicken, it is actually a wild bird that lives in Southeast Asia. There is, however, a good reason that the red junglefowl looks like a chicken—it is the ancestor of the chicken. In prehistoric times, people captured and raised junglefowl for food. Gradually—through a process called domestication—these captured birds became the modern chicken.

People have domesticated other galliforms, such as turkeys, as well. Farmers often breed domestic animals for favorable traits. For example, many farmers allowed only the largest turkeys to breed. Over time, this led to domestic turkeys being much larger than their wild relatives.

Today, millions of chickens and turkeys are raised on farms. They outnumber their wild relatives.

Red junglefowl

Is a Chicken's Comb Cool?

All chickens have a fleshy growth called a comb on the top of their head. Combs are usually more noticeable on males than on females, but all chickens have one. Combs are nearly always red.

Some experts believe that a comb helps a chicken to cool down. When humans are too hot, glands in the skin make sweat. As the sweat evaporates, it cools the skin and the blood that circulates beneath it. A chicken cannot sweat. But, the blood that circulates through the comb cools faster than the blood that circulates in the bird's body. So a chicken sends more blood to its comb when it needs to cool down. The cooler blood that results helps the bird to lower its body temperature.

Combs come in many shapes. The simple, red comb seen often on roosters in cartoons is called a single comb. Some breeds of chickens, such as the Polish, have a V-shaped comb surrounded by an elaborate crest of feathers. Still other chickens have a small comb shaped like a walnut.

Polish rooster

Are Quail and Other Galliforms in Danger?

The heath hen was a kind of grouse found in parts of the United States. It became extinct, or died out, in the 1930's, primarily because so much of its habitat was lost that it could not survive. Some other galliforms may be in danger of becoming extinct, too.

The main danger to galliforms is the activities of people. Towns and cities spread into areas that were once wild grasslands and woodlands. These habitats had made good homes for such animals as quail.

Farmers sometimes use chemicals called pesticides *(PEHS tuh sydz)* to kill harmful insects in their fields. But the chemicals kill all kinds of insects. Quail and other birds are sometimes unable to find enough insects to feed their hungry young.

When large mowers cut an alfalfa field or tall grass on the side of a road, the mowers can chop up the quail nests and eggs hidden in the vegetation. Many young quail are saved when the mowing of fields and roadsides is delayed until the quail nesting season is over, but this practice is not always followed.

Gambel's quail

Galliform Fun Facts

→ Quail, pheasant, and grouse parents sometimes "put on an act" to protect their young. A parent may pretend to be hurt or crippled to draw a hungry animal's attention away from its chicks.

→ A female quail lays her eggs days apart, but they all hatch at the same time. Quail chicks can hear each other while still inside their eggs. They make "click-click" sounds to tell the other chicks when they are ready to hatch.

→ Some grouse fly into snowdrifts at bedtime. The light, fluffy snow makes a good blanket.

→ Long ago, Chinese soldiers believed that brown-eared pheasants were brave and strong. The soldiers wore feathers from this bird when they went into battle.

→ Gambel's quail eat the fruit of the prickly pear cactus. The juice from the fruit stains their faces bright red.

Glossary

brood Sitting on eggs to hatch them; also, a group of newly hatched birds.

camouflage Features of an animal that help it blend into its surroundings.

comb Flap of featherless, brightly colored skin on top of the head of chickens and certain other birds.

covey A small flock, or group, of galliform birds.

crop A baglike swelling on a bird's throat where food is stored.

display When a male bird shows off its brightly colored feathers, or some other feature, to attract a female bird.

fan Feathers on a bird's back that the bird can flatten and spread out like an open fan.

forage To search for food.

game birds Birds that are hunted for sport and meat.

gizzard A muscular part of a bird's digestive system where food is ground up by bits of gravel.

hereditary Refers to traits of an animal that come from the animal's parents.

parasite An organism that feeds and lives on the body of another organism, often causing harm.

pesticide A chemical that is used to kill insects.

predator An animal that hunts and eats other animals.

roost For a bird to rest or sleep; also, the place where a bird rests or sleeps.

ruff A collar of feathers around the neck of some birds.

train Long, colorful feathers that grow from the back of a peacock.

wattle A long, loose piece of skin that hangs from the throat of male turkeys, chickens, and certain other birds.

Index

For more information about Quail and Other Galliforms, try these resources:

Extraordinary Chickens, by Stephen Green-Armytage, Harry N. Abrams, 2000.

Ruffed Grouse: Woodland Drummer, by Michael Furtman, NorthWord Press, 2000.

Peacocks, by Ruth Berman, Lerner Publications, 1996.

http://animaldiversity.ummz.umich.edu/site/accounts/classification/Galliformes.html#Galliformes

http://www.mbr-pwrc.usgs.gov/id/framlst/i2950id.html

Galliform Classification

Scientists classify animals by placing them into groups. The animal kingdom is a group that contains all the world's animals. Phylum, class, order, and family are smaller groups. Each phylum contains many classes. A class contains orders, an order contains families, and a family contains individual species. Each species also has its own scientific name. (The abbreviation "spp." after a genus name indicates that a group of species from a genus is being discussed.) Here is how the animals in this book fit into this system.

Animals with backbones and their relatives (Phylum Chordata)
Birds (Class Aves)
Quail and Other Galliforms (Order Galliformes)
Guineafowl (Family Numididae)

Helmeted guineafowl . . . .*Numida meleagris*

Quail and their relatives (Family Phasianidae)

Black grouse . . . .*Tetrao tetrix* *
Black partridge, or francolin . . . .*Francolinus francolinus*
Blue grouse . . . .*Dendragapus obscurus* *
Brown-eared pheasant . . . .*Crossoptilon mantchuricum*
Bulwer's pheasant . . . .*Lophura bulweri*
Chukar . . . .*Alectoris chukar*
Crested quails . . . .*Callipepla* spp.
    California quail . . . .*Callipepla californica* * *
    Gambel's quail . . . .*Callipepla gambelii* * *
European quail . . . .*Coturnix coturnix*
Golden pheasant . . . .*Chrysolophus pictus*
Gray partridge . . . .*Perdix perdix*
Indian peafowl . . . .*Pavo cristatus*
Junglefowl . . . .*Gallus* spp.
    Domestic chicken . . . .*Gallus gallus domesticus*
    Red junglefowl . . . .*Gallus gallus*
Northern bobwhite . . . .*Colinus virginianus* * *
Prairie-chicken . . . .*Tympanuchus* spp. *
Ptarmigans . . . .*Lagopus* spp. *
Ring-necked pheasant . . . .*Phasianus colchicus*
Ruffed grouse . . . .*Bonasa umbellus* *
Spruce grouse . . . .*Falcipennis canadensis*

Turkeys (Family Meleagrididae)

Wild turkey . . . .*Meleagris gallopavo*

*Scientists often classify certain grouse, prairie-chickens, and ptarmigans into their own family, Tetraonidae.
* *Scientists often classify the northern bobwhite, Gambel's quail, and other New World quail into their own family, Odontophoridae.